EVALUATION:

Whole Language, Whole Child

JANE BASKWILL   **PAULETTE WHITMAN**

SCHOLASTIC

Toronto • Sydney • New York • London • Auckland

For mostly Margaret,
who'll always be Daisy to me.
J.B.

To Kim,
who started out as a friend and became much more.
P.W.

Edited by Adrian Peetoom
Cover by Jo Huxley

Scholastic-TAB Publications Ltd.
123 Newkirk Road, Richmond Hill, Ontario, Canada L4C 3G5

Scholastic Inc.
730 Broadway, New York, NY 10003, USA

Ashton Scholastic Limited
165 Marua Road, Panmure, PO Box 12328, Auckland , New Zealand

Ashton Scholastic Pty Limited
P.O. Box 579, Gosford, NSW 2250, Australia

Scholastic Publications Ltd.
Holly Walk, Leamington Spa, Warwickshire CV32 4LS, England

ISBN 0-590-71858-4

9 8 7 6 5 4 3   Printed in Hong Kong   9/8 0 1 2 3 4/9

Contents

Introduction: science vs. common sense

- You've given a test and most of your children have done poorly.
- You've received a diagnostic report on a problem child, but it adds nothing to what you'd already figured out, and recommends far less than what you're already trying.
- You've administered an end-of-the-book basal reader test and discovered that the one child you *know* had trouble reading the stories has scored very well — while one of your star readers scored very poorly on the same test!
- You've sent a report card home but you have a sinking feeling it doesn't reflect how the child is actually doing.

If you've experienced even one of these situations, you're already very much aware that assessment and evaluation are laced with problems and dilemmas. It isn't as easy as it may seem to record information about children's *real* learning and report it meaningfully to fellow teachers, parents and administrators.

But there is hope. As teachers continue to find out more about teaching and learning, they are developing better tools for evaluating children's work and designing better means of reporting their findings. Current thinking reflects the belief that learning is an individual process which occurs most effectively within a supportive environment — an ongoing process that can't be fragmented or timetabled. Our evaluating tools and methods should also reflect that belief.

Evaluation has always had a touchy side. Everyone accepts that some kinds of learning are difficult to measure, and that some of the less tangible areas of growth, such as self-concept and attitude, elude assessment attempts completely. But we've been led to believe that there are accurate, meaningful tools and methods that make evaluation objective and scientific. Even worse, since many of those methods require experts to design them and special training to administer them, we've been persuaded that reliable conclusions are beyond the scope of regular classroom teachers.

Personally we've found many of the traditional tools cumbersome, others time-consuming. And most of them didn't give us the information we needed to help individual children. We had sorting problems, filing problems, accessing problems. We began to stack up the impressive looking official reports resulting from the more clinical approach against what we saw and felt. We realized we'd become unsure of our own common sense observations and interpretations of what our children were doing, and began to ask ourselves some questions: Who knows our children best? Who is in the best position to make accurate observations and interpretations of what they are doing on a daily, weekly or monthly basis? Who can best interpret their growth in competency over time and collect samples to document it?

We set aside our doubts and began to record and report what we saw our children do and what we heard them say. We might not always understand why something was happening, but we could at least record it and think about it. We could use our common sense, have confidence in our own teaching experience, talk to colleagues, and keep our eyes on professional literature that might help us.

As we gradually developed and became better whole language teachers, we also became more confident and effective observers and interpreters. There *were* alternatives to end-of-the-book tests and standardized testing procedures, we discovered, useful and manageable alternatives that were neither difficult nor complicated, although they required practice and self-discipline to make them most effective.

We've found the switch to a more personal method of evaluation good for both our children and ourselves. We know the children better and are able to meet their needs more effectively. We've become better interpreters of their learning growth and better communicators of that information to their parents. We've become better teachers.

We want to share some of our ideas with you. We hope you'll try several and *not* rely on just one! Choose the ones that suit you best for the moment and give yourself time to grow into the others. With a little time and practice, you'll find evaluation isn't as overwhelming as it's often made out to be.

The early grades: getting the picture

The holistic view of literacy learning has a firm foothold in the early grades, and many teachers are already using new tools to recognize and evaluate the development and growth of their children. In doing so, they are getting a better picture of the whole child. The procedures we describe are some of the many tried and tested over the last few years.

Anecdotal records

We are strong believers in collecting information on each child — the children's work itself, and our notes that record the interactions we observe between one child and print and between one child and other children. Anecdotal recording took practice on our part, but the more we did of it, the better we became. We had to train and constantly remind ourselves to look at the positive, at what the children *could* do. It had been so easy in the past to write down or show examples of what each child could *not* do. We found we were looking at our children with different eyes.

The payoff was rich. The more we looked, the more we saw. And the more we saw, the more we understood what was going on, not only with individual children, but with the class as a whole. So many things which before had gone unnoticed until sometime after the fact were now being observed and recorded as they happened: the day a child wrote her first word using invented spelling, read independently for the first time, made her first book. We were reminded of the first time our own offspring at home took their first steps, said their first words, lost their first teeth. With the same excitement we became first-hand observers of the literacy milestones of our students. And, just as we had as proud parents, we wanted to share the children's firsts with anyone who would listen!

To get into the habit of observing and recording information, we found we had to create specific opportunities. A good look at our daily schedule helped. For instance, independent practice time, when the children were involved in self-selected activities at a variety of centers within the classroom, seemed the perfect time to zero in on what particular children were saying and doing and to record what we were observing.

date	child's name	comment
11/21	Maria	wrote "I cn sat." (I can skate) by herself during writing time.
11/21	Matthew	built a tower of blocks using two colors in ABAB pattern
11/22	Gwen	G.'s mother came to school today. Said G. was making lots of books at home – likes hearing stories – pleased w/ "progress" she sees.

At first we needed to schedule our observing, to ensure that no child was left out and that nothing would get in the way of the commitment we had made. We began by following one child for an entire independent practice session, switching to a new child each day, until we were satisfied we were concentrating on the "can do's." Focusing on one child for an extended period made it possible to think very carefully about what we were observing. What was the child actually demonstrating?

After we felt more secure, we tried recording information about various children each day as something noteworthy developed. Sometimes we found ourselves recording interesting information we weren't really sure would be significant. Yetta Goodman's articles on "kid-watching" helped us focus on important events. We always checked back over what we'd written at the end of the week to see who may have been left out or what patterns seemed to be emerging.

The next question was how to record and store the information we were gathering. Trying out several different ways soon showed us the virtues and limitations of each. We carefully selected those best suited to our own needs, as every teacher must.

File folders

Since accessibility to our anecdotal information is important, before school opens we prepare a file folder for each child coming into our class. Into those files, over the year, go samples of writing and art work; lists of books read, books published and projects undertaken; reports; posters — any useful examples of the children's work. We include work in progress as well as finished products, as an indication of the process the children go through in striving to accomplish specific tasks. We also put in photocopies of interesting journal entries that give us insight into what the children understand about the reading or writing process, or about a science or math concept. We carefully date each item, using a date stamp we keep handy on our desk.

Monthly writing samples

In addition, we ask the children for a monthly writing sample. We ask them to write on a topic of their choice for fifteen minutes, entirely on their own, setting the same safe, comfortable, non-threatening tone we use during routine personal writing time. We tell them why we want the sample and ask them to show us everything they know how to do when they write. At the end of the fifteen minutes we collect and stamp the samples.

We may decide to have individual conferences before filing the samples. If so, we look at the pieces with the children and make a list of all the things they have demonstrated they can do.

```
dr  mom  Nd  dad
   I  wNt  tow  vst  grandma
towmro   o.k. ?
                        Love
                        Amanda
```

What can Amanda do as a writer?
She
  - can use the format of a letter
  - can use some punctuation (question mark, o.k.)
  - Knows the purpose of a letter
  - knows some standard spelling forms (mom, dad, grandma, love, Amanda)
  - uses capitals in some situations (I, Love, Amanda)
  - uses vowels and consonants with invented spellings
  - comes close to standard (wnt = want ; tow = to)
  - uses appropriate word length and overall look of word (towmro)
  - sees writing as a meaningful activity; writing with a purpose in mind.

As the months go by we can see the growth made by individual children. By the end of the year we have quite a revealing record.

Scrapbooks

Scrapbooks provide another way of filing writing samples so a record of progress is evident. Each child's scrapbook should have at least ten pages — one for each month of school. Next to a piece of writing, in the margin of the scrapbook page, we put a brief "translation" if the text is by very young children, a comment about the circumstances that led to the writing, or a note describing further developments of the piece. On the back of each page we write a brief explanation of what the piece tells us about the child's growth in competence. Each sample is dated.

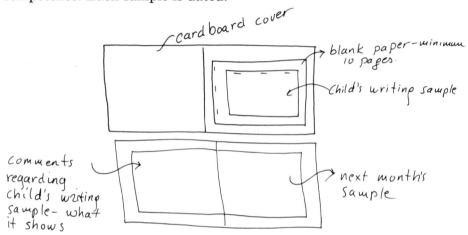

Some of our colleagues pass the scrapbook on to the child's next teacher. We prefer to send it home first, with a suggestion that the parents send it back in the fall. This gives us additional practice in clarifying our observations to ourselves and putting them in a form parents are able to understand. Moreover, it gives the parents a reference point for watching their child's further writing development and encourages contact with the school early in the following year.

Gummed notes

When we needed a quick means of recording the observations we were making during independent practice time, we purchased a roll of gummed address labels. For each observation we wrote the date and the name of the child on a label, along with our comments. Since the labels didn't offer a lot of space for long-winded recording, we quickly learned to be concise, putting down only the important details. At the end of the day, we would stick the labels to the inside of the appropriate file folders, thus providing a chronological record, in one location, of our observations about each child.

Then a problem arose. As we became better observers we discovered that our observations of a particular incident often involved more than one child. Whose folder should we put it in? Should we write additional ones for each of the other children? We also found ourselves recording snippits of a conversation or intricacies of a situation that required more space than one small label gave us. We toyed with the idea of having a number of different sized labels, but envisaged ourslves becoming walking label dispensers who would swamp desks (our own!) with sticky notes that needed filing!

Spiral notebook

So we began carrying with us a spiral notebook we called our "teacher's log." It has become one of the best tools we have for gathering and recording information — and not only about the children. It contains our reflections, our questions, our concerns about particular children or events. It has become a way to think on paper about our observations, to watch relationships and developments reveal themselves. We have the space to write entire conversations if we wish, or to write a description of a complete moment-in-time that seems important. We can quickly look back and check on an entry previously made, and we have ready access to anecdotes to share with parents who might come to school unexpectedly.

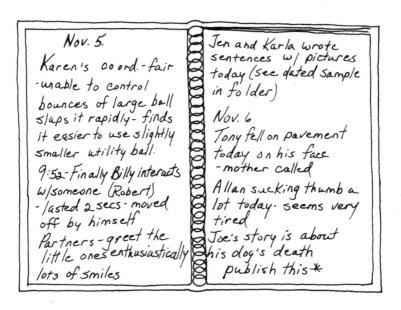

We realize it was fortunate that we didn't begin with a notebook — we needed to learn how to observe first, to practice on the short bits, the obvious moments. But now that we're more established kid-watchers, we find our teacher's log an indispensible item in our evaluative tool kit. At the end of each week we go over all the entries, highlighting or underlining with colored pencil the significant bits of information we want to have at our fingertips. These we transfer onto address labels, along with the date, and put them into the children's folders. Often we add a comment, indicate a plan of action, or make a judgment about what we think is happening. We may also include a sample of the child's work that illustrates our observation.

Bob Wortman, a friend and colleague from Tucson, Arizona, has eliminated the need for transcription by designing an efficient anecdotal record form on which he collects such information. As well as describing the incident itself, he records the date, the setting and the participants. After several anecdotes have been recorded, the forms can be cut apart and glued into individual folders for each child, thus forming a permanent growth record while eliminating the need for transcription.

	Incident	Implications
Name		
Name		

The point is, there is no one right way — you'll develop your own ways of recording the results of your kid-watching. It will be up to you to both record and use the information in the way that's most beneficial to you and your children.

Audio records

Audio cassettes can also provide fine records of reading development. Three times a year we put a sample of each child's reading on an individual cassette, marking the date and the running numbers for each sample. We ask the children to read any story they choose first, and then one we select. In this way we collect both their fluent reading of familiar material and an unrehearsed reading that demonstrates their use of reading strategies on more difficult or unfamiliar text. As we listen, we make notes on the behavior we observe during the reading. Do the children make use of picture clues? Do they do any eye-ear-voice matching? Are they able to handle unknown words without wanting help?

Before we take the samples, we let the children know what we're doing, explaining that we want to hear how they would read a story if no one was around to help. We ask them to pretend they are reading aloud to themselves, or to younger brothers or sisters, with no one else nearby. We try whatever it takes to make them as comfortable as possible and as secure as they'd be in any other risk-taking situation in our classroom. We don't want them to feel they are being tested, or that we expect them to perform in any particular way.

Audio cassettes come in handy when providing examples or explaining points to parents. We can let them hear the differences in the kinds of reading their children do and help them understand the importance and value of those differences. Parents often have difficulty accepting memory reading as legitimate reading, nor do they always understand how children can be orally fluent in one context and not in another. A tape can be a good way to help those parents understand what they are hearing at home.

Tapes also provide a record of progress. By the end of the year parents may have forgotten where their children began, and by sharing their children's readings with them, you can address any unreasonable expectations. Finally, individual tapes can be passed on to each child's next teacher, who will benefit from hearing the preceding year's development.

One word of caution, however — one we keep in mind for every type of evaluation. Never base all your opinions on a single reading sample. Always use recorded readings in conjunction with other information gathered daily.

Video records

Video cassettes have also proved to be effective evaluative tools. By using a video camera to record our children's reading samples, we collect not only an accurate audio record but a visual one as well. We can see how the book is held, where the eyes are looking, whether the page is turned on cue, etc. We still take notes as the children read, but now we have a way of stimulating our memories and interpreting the notes we've taken.

Videotapes also provide a wonderful way of demonstrating to parents what their children are doing when they read, and we can be specific with our examples. We can even pause the tape so the parents can have a better look at what is happening, or so we can make a particular point or add information. We can't afford a separate tape for each child, but it's easy to note and record the footage as each child reads. Our children are quite used to being videotaped and are now as natural on camera as off.

At times we might record the children during independent practice time and personal writing time, perhaps to show a particular child's interaction with others, or concentration on task. Once again, these tapes provide us with an excellent basis for talks with parents about their children.

Conference binder

We use a three-hole looseleaf binder for an ongoing record of the regular readings the children do with us from self-selected and teacher-selected materials.

We try to tune in to each child at least twice a week. With some we might tune in daily, at least for a certain period of time. These sessions are mini-conferences in which we talk freely about using particular strategies and help the children use them. They usually take no more than three to five minutes per child, but are very effective in helping the children gain independence (see chapter six in Don Holdaway's *Foundations Of Literacy*).

In the binder we record the selection read and describe how the child used a particular strategy, or what we worked on. Each entry is dated. A tab for each child makes the location of individual records easy. By the end of the year we have accumulated a complete record of how we worked with individual children, what we perceived their needs to be, and how they responded to strategy sessions.

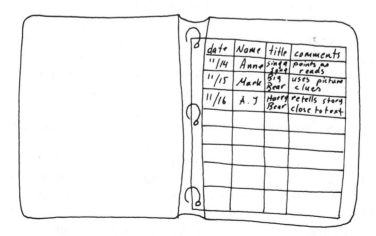

Preschool profiles

So far we've been talking about gathering daily, weekly and monthly information as we work with the children, and about collecting samples and recording observations. We also find it helpful to gather information that might shed light on the children's past literacy development.

Registration: the child

Spring registration is usually the first opportunity you have to find out something about next year's group of children.

Traditionally in our area, as in most, the children and at least one parent were invited to the school well in advance to provide health records and an indication of "readiness skills" such as coloring, counting and drawing, and recognizing the alphabet, colors and shapes. The results of those "tests" were then filed to be used by the kindergarten/primary teacher in the fall. However, the information was seldom used. Instead, teachers did their own informal assessments once the children were settled into school. In the worst cases, registration tests were used to label children and divide them into "high" and "low" groups, perhaps even separating them into different classes. We now know that children labeled this way often live up to expectations, seldom moving out of the stream they were originally placed in.

This kind of registration can be very disturbing for both parents and children — making both feel like failures. Besides, information collected under such circumstances is generally of very little help to teachers with a holistic philosophy. Checklists of supposed readiness skills aren't valid indicators of children's literacy development, since they don't accurately reflect the development that has already taken place. Teachers need to know how the children interact with print, what they understand reading and writing to be, how they feel about books and stories, and how much they've been read to at home.

As a result, our primary registration takes a different approach. We invite individual parents and children to come to school together at a scheduled hour, and arrange parental permission to videotape the interview. When they arrive, we leave the child to look around the room and get acquainted with things (we make sure there are three or four colorful children's books on the table) while we talk briefly with the parents and ask them to fill out the forms required by our public health department. Then we ask the child to come sit next to us while we read aloud whichever book he chooses. As we read, we involve him by talking about the pictures and the story as naturally as possible and, if appropriate, inviting a read-along.

This brief sharing gives us some idea of the child's language development, enjoyment of stories and understanding of the specific story as it relates to a familiar incident in his life. The responses can be very revealing to the parents, who will overhear the discussion we have with the child. The situation isn't threatening to either child or parents, and it often sparks the parents' curiosity about our reasons for gathering such information. We hope the resulting conversation will be the first of many with the parents, especially about the importance of their role.

Next we ask the child to draw us a picture. We have a variety of writing implements on the table — crayons, pencils, colored pencils, thin and fat markers — along with several different kinds of paper. The child selects the paper and the tool(s) he wants to use. Many things are revealed to us as we observe the drawing in progress: some children talk about what they are drawing; some add sound effects as part of the action; some, who obviously have done very little drawing, are unsure how to start. Once again as we talk with the child about what he is doing we learn from his responses and from the language he uses to talk about his drawings.

Finally we ask the child to write something for us. Few children hesitate to pick up a pencil or pen and write letters, names, numbers, words posted on the wall, etc. This gives us a good idea of writing development and print awareness. Some children may say they can't write, but they can usually be persuaded to try if we ask them to write us a message. After the child writes the message, we ask him to read it to us, a simple activity that serves to give us a wealth of information we were simply not gathering in the past.

We will also have the videotape to play later so we can make some notes for the fall, either on sticky labels to be put in the child's folder, or in our teacher's log. Long before school starts we already have a good insight into each child's literacy development.

Registration: the parents

While the child is looking around and getting acquainted with the classroom, we take the opportunity to survey the parents' attitude toward reading, and their understanding of the reading/writing process. For that we've developed a "parent survey" form.

Both their attitude and their understanding can have an important effect on our efforts to communicate about our program and their child's progress over the year. They can also give us an important insight into how the child's literacy development has been influenced so far.

PARENT SURVEY

1. Do you consider yourself a good reader? _____

2. What do you like to read? _____

_____

3. How often would _____ see you reading?

☐ every day

☐ frequently

☐ occasionally

☐ never

Tests and checklists

Slightly more formal tests can give you excellent information about the children, and checklists can help you in your observations.

Concept about print tests

Marie Clay and David Doake have both developed "concept about print" tests that yield information about children's book handling knowledge. A similar one, by Yetta Goodman and Bess Altwerger, can be found in the *Bookshelf* Stage 1 Teacher's Resource Book. Besides being useful for surveying incoming kindergarten/primary children, these tests can be administered to young at-risk readers who may be struggling in grade one programs.

Item	Administration	Instruction	Response	Child's response
1	Show book; title covered by hand. Flip over pages	'What's this called?' 'What's this thing?' If child answers with the name of the book, record and ask 'What's (say name of book given by child)?'	'Book', 'Story book', 'Story', Name of book	
2	Displaying book	'What do you do with it?'	'Read it', 'Look at it', 'Tell it', 'Open it'	
3	Displaying book	'What's inside it?'	'Story', 'Picture', 'Words', 'Pages', 'Letters', 'Things'	
4	Present book wrong way up and back towards child	'Show me the front of this book', 'Take the book and open it so that we can read it together'	Any indication of front or first page	
5	Turn to page 3	Hold on to a page and say 'Show me a page in this book', 'Is this a page?'	Points to page; 'Yes'	
6	Give the book to child	Read this to me	[Record all responses]	

Self-concept tests

Some teachers find it useful to administer one of several tests on the market to get an overall picture of how the children feel about themselves and their relationships with others.

Sight words tests

At some point you may want to determine what basic sight words the children know. In *Independence in Reading*, Don Holdaway includes a list of such words and a means for determining whether the children know them outright (that is, out of context), or if not, if they can determine them within context. A totally different picture of basic sight word recognition is presented when contextual use is included.

The Holdaway list is also the basis of a computer-assisted drill of basic sight words developed by Steve Baskwill. Once the teacher has chosen the words to be presented, the program allows the child, or a teacher aide, to call up the word in context. The program can be used by the teacher to administer a basic sight words test or by the children as a drill of the words they don't know or know only within context.

Literacy skills checklists

First, a warning about checklists: no matter what you do with them, the fact that they are written in a linear, sequential fashion often misleads people into thinking that is the order in which things must happen. Unfortunately, they are often viewed as lists from which to teach.

Yet checklists can be useful. They can help you learn to observe children by making you aware of the kinds of things you should be looking for, and can provide yet another way for you to record the information you gather. It has been our experience that checklists are often long and somewhat cumbersome; in an attempt to provide help, their designers try to include everything. Even so, they can give you a good detailed picture of what to expect from your children as they pass through the major developmental reading and writing phases.

In our area, each school district has been left to develop its own checklist, should it feel one is needed. Our provincial language arts guide includes a list of observable behaviors divided into three stages of literacy development: early literacy, transitional literacy and independent literacy. These, along with charts outlining expectations at the grade 2, 4 and 6 levels, provide districts with a nice starting point for developing their own lists. Such checklists are meant as guidelines, not as prescriptions for teaching. A child's development cannot be fragmented or timetabled. The expectations are broad in scope so children will be given the time necessary to achieve them.

There are also several publishers' checklists available as part of newly developed whole language programs. The following have reading and writing development checklists as part of their teaching manuals or resource books:

- *Bookshelf*, an Australian program available from Scholastic.
- *Impressions*, a Canadian program available from Holt, Rinehart and Winston.
- *Storybox*, a New Zealand program available in Canada from Ginn, in the United States from the Wright Group.
- *A Writing Curriculum: Process and Conference* by Gaelena Rowe and Bill Lomas.

These checklists are designed to be photocopied, and permission for photocopying is included.

After using checklists for a while you may reach the point where you find they are taking more time than they are worth, or you aren't using the information on them, or you are recording more appropriate information in other ways. Then put the lists aside! The most useful checklist will be the one that by then you carry around in your head and use as you observe your children on a daily basis. The prepared checklists will simply have helped you reach that goal.

Miscue analysis

Miscue analysis is a tool you can use to help you understand what strategies a child is employing while reading. It offers a new way of looking at language learning, one not provided by the commonly used informal reading inventory. The actual inventory, developed by Yetta Goodman and Carolyn Burke, is extremely valuable for resource teachers, diagnosticians and teachers in a position to take a block of time to administer and score it. But the process is time consuming and almost impossible for the average classroom teacher to use in its original form. The following modification is equally useful, however, and within the capabilities of ordinary teachers.

What you do is record the miscues a child makes while reading a selection orally and the information you get from her retelling of the selection after the first reading. First you make two copies of the selection to be read, one for the child and one for you. Yours should be double-spaced to allow for note taking so that through the use of shorthand marks that designate the kind of miscues made you can record what the child does and says while reading. It's useful to tape the reading as well so you can go back and add any miscues you overlooked during the session. Then you can look at the quality or type of errors made and the frequency of each.

- Was the child working for meaning?
- Did her miscues retain meaning or disrupt it?
- What did she do when she came to an unknown word?
- Was she over-attending to the physical appearance of individual words?
- Was she making too much use of phonic decoding skills at the expense of meaning?
- Did she skip too many words without attempting to tackle them? If so, did this affect her retelling of the story?

I was walking down the road

Then I saw a little toad
(frog written above "toad", toad crossed with correction)

corrected to toad

catched
I caught it.

Then
I picked it up,

box
I put it in a cage

    The way you interpret what the child does will reflect what you understand reading to be. For instance, if she reads the word *feather* for *father*, a phonics-oriented teacher might be pleased because she's come close to sounding the word out. However, if you believe reading is a meaning-seeking process, you may be concerned that she's overly dependent on phonics at the expense of meaning. You'd be happier with a miscue such as *daddy*, even though it doesn't look or sound anything like the word in the text. At least the meaning would be intact.

    Miscue analysis gives you the information to make important observations and ultimate decisions regarding a child's stage of reading development. Even using simplified miscue and retelling forms like those in the *Impressions* Teacher Resource Books can be very effective. As you become more proficient and gain experience using miscue analysis, you'll find that the way you listen to children reading will change. You'll notice yourself doing mental, on-the-spot analyses in most cases and more formal ones only when you need additional information to deal with a troubled reader.

MISCUE RECORDING CHECKLIST

Name _____ Date _____

Selection _____

Put a checkmark in the appropriate column when the child makes a miscue.
Circle the checkmark if the child notices the miscue and attempts to correct it.

✓
⊘

Type of miscue	Miscues resulting in no loss of meaning ("home" for "house")	Miscues resulting in loss of meaning ("house" for "horse")
Substitution		
Omission		
Insertion		
Repetition		
Reversal		

Summary:

Total number of miscues _____

Miscues resulting in no loss of meaning _____

Miscues resulting in loss of meaning _____

Correction attempts _____

Comments: _____
_____
_____

Standardized tests

There has been and continues to be a lot of debate over the usefulness of standardized tests. Some school boards and districts require them. Some take them so seriously that they publish the results in the local newspaper. But if you must use standardized tests, please see them for what they are: indicators of how well a child took the test on a given day, *not* how well that child reads.

A child brings a lot more to each reading situation than can be measured in one test. The test may claim to give a measure of the child's vocabulary, but as Holdaway has indicated, context is important for vocabulary recognition. The test merely tells you how the child copes with words out of context and with unreal texts.

You should also keep in mind that if you've been using a literature based language program your children may not be used to hearing or reading the language of standardized tests — which can put them at a distinct disadvantage when being tested. We suggest that you take some time before the actual test to give them practice with the test language — not using the actual test, of course, but demonstrating what kinds of questions will be asked and how they should be answered. If out-of-date line drawings are used, as they often are in tests for young readers, be sure to show the children some pictures from older workbooks. You want them to be familiar with the odd-looking upright thing called a vacuum cleaner!

Above all, talk to the children honestly about the test they'll be taking. Don't do it in a negative way — after all, you want them to go into it feeling confident and capable. But you also want them to realize that there'll be both easy parts and hard parts, that you don't expect them to know everything, and that it will be easier for some than for others. Let them know that the test is measuring how well they take the test, not how well they read. Prepare parents ahead of time as well, so they know what test is being given and what it actually measures, as opposed to what it claims to measure.

The upper grades: building on success

So far we've been making reference to the early grades, where whole language classrooms are fairly common and whole language teachers aware of the need for more effective evaluation techniques. But the need is just as great in the upper elementary grades, and the main purposes of evaluation the same:

- to discover how we can help each child achieve more;
- to assess the validity and effectiveness of our program;
- to communicate a child's progress as fully as we can to the parents and other teachers.

Do your current procedures answer those objectives? If they don't, or if you honestly don't know, perhaps you're ready to consider some changes. You'll find many suggestions to choose from in this chapter, but if you skipped the first chapter because you teach in the upper grades, we ask you to go back and read it as well. Rethinking evaluation has just begun at the higher levels and substantial progress will be made only if upper elementary teachers absorb what is already there in the early grades, then work at refining and expanding.

More and more, teachers in the upper grades are beginning to watch literacy learners in action, tuning in to the *process* of literacy learning and discovering more about how children really learn to read and write at various ages. Like their colleagues in the early grades, they are catching on to this notion: learners learn much the same way at any age. Learners learn most easily the material they are interested in, stuff that's meaningful to them. They learn best in a safe, supportive environment in which risk-taking is encouraged. They learn quickest when they engage in self-initiated practice and when they see individuals they trust engaged in the same tasks. With that in mind, many teachers are beginning to recognize the limitations and shortcomings of some of the evaluative tools they've been used to using. How can such learning be assessed by a meaningless system of letters or numbers which are at best arbitrary and at worst counterproductive to an individual's learning attempts?

While a growing number of publications and programs are already available to provide general help at the upper elementary level (see Bibliography), we must realize that the profession has only begun to rethink its evaluation methods. Teachers at this level are in for an exciting future as professional colleagues and researchers respond to the urgent evaluation questions being asked by educators everywhere. But we want to sound a note or two of caution: don't overwhelm yourself by immediately trying to do everything you read or hear about. Give yourself time to become familiar with new evaluative tools. Try a limited number at a time and trust yourself to choose those most appropriate and effective for your purposes. And remember that changes — *real* changes — in education will happen only if teachers take responsibility for their own classroom decisions. Don't wait for the "perfect" tools to be produced by someone else for you to imitate.

Learning profiles

All teachers would like to have as much information as they can about their children on the first day of school. But a file folder full of grades and marks passed on from last year's teacher really doesn't say much about how the children learn, what they know already, and how you can best help them: the heart of our evaluation philosophy.

It often takes a while to get to know your children, but creating learning profiles early in the school year will speed up the process. Such profiles provide insight into the strategies the children are using, and their attitude toward their own development. Sometimes the information you get will simply make you aware that you need to know more; other times it will open the door to understanding specific instructional needs. Unfortunately, learning profiles can't give you a complete picture of the children's previous literacy development. You'll still have only part of the picture. But it's an important part. It will give you a starting point. Instead of having to wait months to know your children and understand their needs, you'll be able to interact with them in a personal and meaningful fashion from the first weeks of school.

Although beginning the year this way involves time and planning, the benefits are worth the effort and many teachers we know happily make the time. Some put off beginning any formal language program for several weeks, simply providing the children with a variety of reading materials and the opportunity to select and read at will while they work with individual children to create the profiles.

It's best to conduct surveys and issue questionnaires on an individual basis, but you may find it necessary to distribute them in printed form to the class as a whole, discussing responses with individual children at a later date. Or you may decide to borrow an hour a week from other curriculum areas — after all, literacy development isn't limited to one area of the curriculum. It's part of all we do, both in and out of school.

Reading

You might begin collecting reading profiles by administering a Burke Reading Interest Survey, which will provide insights into the children's interests and attitudes about reading. Its questions elicit information about what the children like to read, feel about reading, and understand about the reading process. You may also want to make a tape recording of each child reading, first a self-selected piece and then a piece you have chosen.

There are other surveys available as well, such as the personal interest record in the *Three I's* program, which can serve as a first step in getting to know your children's interests. You may already have one you use, or you may want to design one that suits your needs.

Of course it takes time to develop this kind of comprehensive profile, but it is time well invested. You'll get a good deal of useful knowledge about each child and an immediate base of information to help you prepare for conferences, recommend books the children might like to read, and figure out how you can best help guide their development as readers.

| **Personal Interest Record** | Name _____ |
| | Date _____ |

My family (including pets) _____

_____

_____

_____

My height _____ My weight _____

My best friends _____

_____

What interests me most _____

Writing

Also include writing samples in your profile. Ask the children to write sample pieces, explaining that you'll use them to learn how they write and how you, as a teacher, can help them write better. Explain that they should try to show you all they know how to do when they write: using capitals, punctuation, titles, interesting leads, etc. Remind them to be careful of their spelling, but if they're not sure of a word, to spell it as best they can. You can take samples from the whole class at the same time by allowing fifteen minutes and then collecting the pieces, even if they're not finished.

As soon as possible, meet with each child individually and together develop a list of the skills demonstrated. Make two copies of the list, one for the child's writing folder and one for you to keep with the writing sample. You may also want to ask if there's any other writing skill the child would like to show you he can use. Give him an opportunity to demonstrate, and add that sample to the other. Writing samples can be taken in this fashion each month and compared over time.

Remember, these first writing samples won't give you a complete picture of the children's writing abilities. They're only a beginning. As your writing program develops, you'll have many writing conferences and collect many writing samples. Don't be alarmed if you notice the children aren't using particular skills that were apparent in previous samples. They may have become so involved in their writing or been so busy trying to demonstrate a new skill that they forgot to use the old one. Be patient. Don't jump the gun and become concerned without due cause. Learning and growth take place over time.

Spelling

You may also want to add spelling information to the children's profiles. The purpose isn't to find out how many words they can spell correctly, but to gain insight into the strategies they use.

- What cueing systems are they using? What kinds of errors are they making?
- How do they react when they're not sure how to spell a word?
- Are they demonstrating a knowledge of spelling conventions?
- What patterns can be found in their misspellings?

You can find some of the answers to these questions by asking the children to write a list of not more than twenty words as you dictate them. First explain why you're doing it: it's not a test, but a way for you to help them become better spellers. Remind them that you are not concerned about the number of right or wrong spellings, and encourage them to try the words as best they can. Explain that although you won't help them spell the words, you will give them the meanings if they wish. Choose words you feel are somewhere between "too easy" and "too challenging" and give them both in isolation and in context. Afterwards, sit down with each child and go over the list together. Ask such questions as:

- Which words do you think you spelled correctly?
- Which ones aren't you sure about?
- Why did you decide on this particular spelling?
- How else could you have tried to spell this word?
- If this word is incorrect, how could you find the correct spelling?

Anecdotal records

All the suggestions we made earlier about keeping anecdotal records for younger children can be just as effective for assessing the progress of your older students. Jot down your observations: the books they choose; any remarks that give you insight into their interests, their thinking or their competencies; their use of reading and writing strategies; etc. Keep a notebook handy for putting down anything and everything that might be of interest later.

At first you may find this more difficult than teachers in the early grades do. You may find that although you've been attuned to *what* the children read and write, you haven't been aware of what they *do* as they read and write. Soon you'll begin to see things differently.

- You tune in to those children who never seem to finish a book, who begin many but move on to another before completing the one they've started.
- You notice those who choose to read only a particular kind of book, books of a particular genre, by a certain author, or recommended by their friends.
- You become aware of the children who are so concerned with neatness, correct spelling and writing conventions that they are virtually unable to transfer their thoughts to paper.

- You observe those who stop their reading at each word they don't know and ask someone nearby for help.
- Over time you begin to recognize subtleties: Sue writes well in narrative form; Bruce's writing seems to focus on topics related to television; Tony becomes less frustrated when given the opportunity to explain how he feels about something; Carrie is beginning to use dialogue in a lot of her writing.

At times you may want to know a lot more about a certain child. Perhaps he isn't progressing as you expected, or is exhibiting frustration with materials that seem appropriate. Perhaps your observations have pointed out inconsistencies. Any of the evaluation tools described earlier will help you achieve greater insight.

Conference logs

If you are using a self-selected individualized reading program and if you conference with your children about their writing, you'll want to keep reading and writing conference logs. In your reading log, a page per child will give you an ongoing comprehensive record of your discussions about the books each child reads. We prefer a large three-ring binder for jotting down interesting comments the children make about a book, reflections on their understanding of what they've read, ideas for possible follow-ups, etc. Your writing log will be similar. Don't feel you have to write reams of information. Comments such as *Discussed opening*, *Wants to publish later*, *Still working on grandfather story*, *Difficulty rereading piece* may be short, but they provide insightful information and reminders of things you might want to check on during your next conference with the child.

Conference Log	Name _____

Book Title _____ Date_____

Comments _____

_____

_____

_____

_____

Checklists

Developmental lists can be found in such publications as *Independence in Reading* by Don Holdaway, *Language Arts in the Elementary School* by the Nova Scotia Department of Education, *Reading, Writing and Caring* by Whole Language Consultants, and teaching guides for various reading programs.

A note of caution: use these lists as guidelines only, not as checks to see who's doing or not doing what. They are very helpful, however, in giving you the language to describe what you see, and most effective when used as a reference. They should serve as a stepping stone in the development of the ultimate checklist: *the one you carry around in your head.* After you become comfortable with the items on the prepared lists, you'll automatically begin to jot down other (your) kinds of observations: questions that arise as you interact with the children, comments that give you insight into their thinking or learning, snippets of your own thoughts and reflections on the observations you record.

Children's work

You may already be in the habit of collecting samples of your children's work: tests, completed stories, book reports, etc. We'd like to suggest a broader range of material from across all curriculum areas. Look for writing samples you feel show evidence of progress and growth: the first time the children try a particular convention or format, an interesting comment or critique written about a book they've read, a copy of a puzzle they've developed, a sketch of something they're planning to build, a list of questions they'd like to research about a theme, a brainstorming, a survey they've developed, a map they've drawn, etc. Sometimes you may find you want to collect pieces still being worked on, ones you feel should be kept just as they are in a writing folder or theme notebook. You can make photocopies of those pieces or put reference numbers on the backs of the originals. Store each child's collection in a folder, noting the contents on the cover.

Don't try to collect everything. Be selective, saving only the pieces you feel provide information about the children's thinking and learning. And don't limit your samples to ones that have been taken to completion — you can get many insights from abandoned beginnings, rough drafts, revisions and experiments. Your purpose isn't to evaluate each piece individually; you simply want to assess growth.

If you use a thematic approach, you may want to have all theme related materials in a theme notebook — for instance, a suitable three-ring binder. Encourage the children to keep all their work together so you can look at their notebooks and observe their progress and development through the theme. Glancing through all the theme books kept by one child will allow you to assess his growth over a long period.

Self-evaluation records

Certain kinds of record keeping provide children with an opportunity to become aware of their own growth and achievements.

Reading logs

Individual reading logs record all the reading the children do. In Scholastic's *Three I's* program a printmaster of such a log has been provided for unlimited duplication.

Reading Log	Name _____

Book Title _____

Author _____ Date _____

Review _____

_____

_____

Recommendation _____

_____

Activity _____

_____

Notes _____

_____

_____

Writing logs

Similar records trace writing development. Don Graves and Lucy McCormick Calkins both suggest that individual children keep an ongoing list of skills they are using competently in their writing. This might be as simple as a sheet of paper stapled to their writing folder and titled *Skills I Can Use, My List of Can Do's, Skills (name of child) Can Use*, etc. As you and the children become aware during conferences of what strategies and skills they are using in their writing, these should be jotted down on the list. The list may include some strategies the children are trying out for the first time, some they've been experimenting with, and some they feel they can use competently.

Learning logs

Another useful record is a learning log, in which the children enter what they've learned: information they've discovered for the first time, a new understanding about the way things work or the connections that link up information, different ways of doing things, etc. This is particularly effective in such areas of the curriculum as science, social studies and mathematics. Such logs provide you with an up-to-the-minute view of how the children are processing what is happening in the classroom and how they are perceiving the information they're receiving. Can they describe what they've learned? Make connections? Organize isolated ideas into meaningful statements?

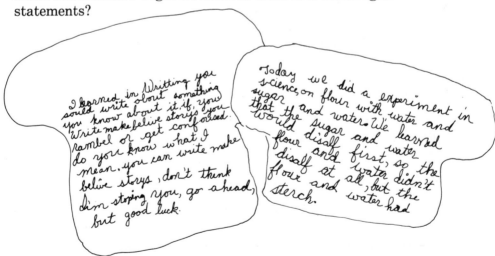

Today I learned that there are many systems in our body. If one of them would not function right, we could get bad illnesss.
In math I learned that when you multiply with a decial by ahundred, you move the decimal forwards as many times there is a zero, and vice versa when dividing. In Science, we talked about force. Everyone in my class stood around the table while a boy was on it and with only useing two fingers each, we lifted him right over our heads!
In social studies, we talked about the Irish and how hard it was for them to settle in Nova Scotia, since they wern't good at farmers.

This kind of recording improves with time as the children come to understand what kinds of things are appropriate to include, how best to say what they want to say, etc. It can become an effective learning tool in itself, not only for the children, but for you as well when you find the messages your children are getting aren't the ones you mean to send at all!

Miscue analysis

Miscue analysis is a valuable tool which can provide you with an in-depth understanding of what strategies the children are using when they read. You shouldn't assume that children in the upper grades are independent readers using reading strategies competently. You still need to tune in to their reading to see which ones they are using and if they're using them effectively. An analysis of their miscues can answer some of the following questions:

- Are they relying too heavily upon one particular strategy?
- When one strategy doesn't work do they give up or try another?
- Are they reading for meaning or are they reading word for word?
- Do they understand what they're reading?

Formal tests

Often at the upper elementary levels, especially in curriculum areas such as science and social studies, bodies of information are discussed, memorized and regurgitated on a test. Projects, special activities and class participation tend to be regarded as supplementary activities. But more and more teachers are questioning the purpose of class testing. Is it to find out what the children have memorized? Is it to check what they don't know? Is it to discover if they understand what's been discussed? Is it to get a mark for the report card?

If you are using tests to evaluate children in subject areas, make sure they reflect your teaching emphases. If indeed all you want to find out is what facts the children know, then give a fact-finding test. But we want to ask you two questions. First, what do you do when they *don't* know the facts you want them to know? Secondly, isn't there a better reason for teaching science and social studies, and therefore a better reason and way to evaluate a particular unit of study?

We'd rather discover if our children understand what they've learned. So we ask questions that require them to *use* the information they've studied. We solicit their opinions, encourage them to reflect on the importance of what they've learned, and require them to use the information in a meaningful way. If properly designed, tests can give insight not only into what children remember, but also into how they perceive, understand and are able to process information.

Much depends on the wording of the questions. Multiple choice, fill in the blank and matching questions don't let us see into the child's mind. We prefer questions that challenge them to think:

- Suppose you . . .
- What do you think might happen if . . .
- If the following facts are true, what do you think . . .
- What would you do if . . .
- If you found yourself in the following situation, what would you . . .
- In light of what you know about . . . , what would you suggest that . . .

Ask the children to give a summary of the most important information about a topic, to defend their statements, to prepare questions about the topic, to tell what they found most interesting, to make lists of materials they need to develop an experiment or a creative representation of a statement or situation. Ask them to develop a poster that gives information about the topic, or write a newspaper article about it. At times you might use some facts from your study to pose a hypothetical question.

In such a test the traditional concept of "ask a question with the purpose of getting a right or wrong answer" seems to have disappeared. Opinions can't be wrong. But interestingly enough, the information and the line of thinking used to develop those opinions can still be evaluated. What you evaluate won't be the number of facts the children have managed to retain, but the way they can use the facts. And this is really what the study of science and social studies is about in the first place.

As we explore the different facets of a subject, our purpose as teachers isn't to have the children come away with a head full of isolated facts. We want them to know how to research for facts, how to find the answers to questions, how to use information to solve problems, make predictions, experiment. If we look back at our own education, we soon realize that very few isolated facts have stayed with us. Those that were meaningful because we connected them to our previous knowledge, those we found useful or interesting, those we actually used in our real lives are the facts we've retained. Those we memorized for a test have long since become history. We had them for a while, but only as long as we had a purpose for keeping them. Once the test was over, most of them disappeared.

If your school reporting system requires you to give a grade or number as a measure of achievement, do so, but on the basis of tests that evaluate the children's ability to *use* information. And a written report should supplement the report card, one that describes the strengths, interests and accomplishments of the children as well as the processes and strategies they are practicing and developing.

Projects

Project work is another facet of the upper elementary program that is usually scrutinized for evaluative purposes. Some teachers find a contractual system an efficient method of involving the children in the evaluative process, and also of keeping track of the necessary recording. In consultation with the teacher, the children decide on the topic and the format of the project, as well as the criteria that will be used to evaluate it. It's wise to make such contracts flexible, however, to provide for a change of interest or plans.

If you decide to assign projects and evaluate them yourself, make sure the children are aware, before they plan and begin work, of the criteria you'll be using to make your evaluation. You can broaden the scope of your evaluation by asking the children to include any rough drafts they did while working on the project. That way you can also make observations about their planning, their revising skills, and their ability to develop an effective presentation of an idea.

As with everything you evaluate, make sure the assessment is a private matter between you and the child. Evaluations should be written on a separate piece of paper that can be attached to the work but removed when the piece is displayed or shared with classmates, parents or visitors. This holds true for good as well as less glowing evaluations. Also make sure that your comments focus on the positive aspects of the work and that constructive criticisms provide helpful suggestions for future work.

One of the problems often encountered at the upper elementary level is difficulty keeping track of what the children are doing, particularly if they're engaged in self-selected activities. The answer doesn't lie in giving more tests or grading more projects, but in devising, implementing and maintaining efficient methods of monitoring. And it doesn't need to take all your time and energy.

As your evaluation of the children becomes a daily occurrence instead of a ritual, you'll get into the habit of keeping your pen handy and your log books accessible. At first you may find you're trying to "get everything down," but gradually you'll become more confident and selective in your recording. With a little planning and regular bookkeeping, your system shouldn't be overwhelming.

Although it may seem time-consuming to begin with, don't give up or let the habit of keeping track gradually disappear. Once you develop a good knowledge of your children and begin to share it with the parents, you'll recognize its impact on your effectiveness as a teacher and its positive influence on your interaction with the children. Continuous evaluation is a habit you won't want to break! Getting in touch with your children is a truly rewarding and beneficial learning experience for both you and the children. No numbers, no letter grades have ever given you that before!

The reporting problem: sharing insights

Do parents and children want grades and marks? Many teachers argue that they do. Without them, they say, some parents don't understand how their children are doing and some children don't bother to work. Parents want to know their children will be okay. They expect — even ask for — numbers or letters because that's the kind of evaluation *they* went through. And especially at the upper elementary levels, many children have already been so indoctrinated into the "marking" process that they seem to feel they can't function without grades.

Our response is simple: in schools where such a system is no longer used, the children are *not* asking for marks and grades, and they are continuing to learn and achieve. Our explanation is equally simple: human beings have been created with a natural drive to learn, and if this drive isn't thwarted, they'll go on learning all their lives.

Another argument given by some upper elementary teachers is that they are preparing the children for the kind of evaluation usually done at the secondary levels. Perhaps, but in doing so they are sacrificing useful information that will help them to work with those children *now* and communicate their progress to parents and other teachers.

The education of children should be the responsibility of both home and school, with insights into the children's ongoing growth and development freely shared. We teachers need to become interpreters, translating our collection of observations and understandings into a meaningful format for parents — one which gives an insightful portrayal of their children's academic and social development.

Just as we've been misled at times into believing that prescribed tests and evaluation tools give us an accurate picture of children's abilities, we've also been persuaded that report cards using numbers or letters are able to give parents a precise and accurate accounting of their children's progress.

But most of us have always been conscious of the shortcomings and ineffectiveness of such reporting devices. We've experienced feelings of frustration and inadequacy as we tried to depict a child's growth and development in terms of *A*, *B*, *S*, or *F*. Such reporting becomes even more confusing when we realize that each teacher has an individual interpretation of such terms as *exceptional, experiencing difficulty* and *fair*. One teacher's *good* may be another's *excellent*. There's also the problem of figuring out which grade to use when the child is good at something sometimes, exceptional at other times, and poor occasionally. To further muddy the waters, teachers have different viewpoints about the number of high and low marks that can be given without the children becoming over-confident or discouraged. The fallacy of thinking it's possible to give a true picture of development in such a fashion becomes obvious and almost embarrassing.

And if teachers are frustrated filling out such a report, how must parents feel trying to make sense of it? Many decide to compare the number of high marks to the number of low. Others decide it's best to compare the number of good or bad marks with the number of similar marks the child received last term, or with the number received by their neighbor's child.

The misunderstanding of the usefulness of this kind of report is even more evident when we see children comparing their marks with friends and summing them up in terms of "Whew!"; "I'm in trouble!"; "You did better than me!"; or "Boy, will Mom be mad!" The very nature of the report stimulates and invites comparison and competition. The children who have passed or gotten straight *A*'s are excited and joyful. But what of those who haven't fared as well, who are labeled as *experiencing difficulty* or *unsatisfactory*? Traditional reporting doesn't even leave room to mention their accomplishments, successes and strengths. Their efforts and gains are lost in the list of numbers and letters, which they may never be able to measure up to. What does this do to their drive, their initiative, their desire to go on?

Besides, of what value to parents is this kind of reporting? Does it give them real insight into their children's development? Does it encourage them to think about learning as an ongoing process or as tiny parcels of sequential information and skills to be mastered and checked off? Does it inspire parents to stress the importance of trying, experimenting and practicing, or does it emphasize failure and competition?

If we admit that our reporting system is ineffective, we should try to do something about it. Sometimes it seems that instead of real alternatives teachers are simply looking for a bag of tricks that will provide them with ready solutions to their evaluating and reporting problems. But for every teacher the "bag of tricks" is different, depending on the situation. We teachers have to take it upon ourselves to devise or demand better reporting systems, something more in keeping with our own experiences and needs and with the needs of our children and their parents. There's no magic to it. Nor is there any easy or fast solution. It takes time and work, but it's our responsibility to do it in the most professional manner possible.

Parents and teachers have long recognized that the most important part of a report card is the space allocated for comments. Usually, however, the limited space restricts any written observations to two or three sentences. Or the teacher's time has been so taken up with providing the letters and numbers required that there's little energy left for putting into comments.

An anecdotal report card is very effective as a reporting device. It's a written report — not just a sentence or two but a meaningful description of a child's development and progress in various curriculum areas. It's as important in creating that kind of report as in recording daily observations of the children to focus on the "can do's." Include what the children can already do well, what strategies they are experimenting with and practicing, and what they might be expected to do in the next few weeks. Your comments must be well articulated and explained so the parents clearly understand what they mean. A poorly written anecdotal report will be of little use, so it's important to train yourself to become the best reporter possible.

If you're apprehensive about writing such reports, begin by sitting down with the files you've created of your children's pieces and your own observations, along with a checklist of "milestones" to use for reference. You may want to pass your first attempt or two on to a colleague, along with the children's work, and ask what that person understands you to be saying. The response might give you insight into how to make what you're trying to report clearer. Although reporting to parents is a private matter, seeking consultation with and support from other teachers is certainly both a professional and a beneficial activity. Just as your ability to make observations and keep anecdotal records of the children's development will improve with practice, so will your ability to write a concise interpretation of your understandings. Don't give up if your first attempts don't meet your expectations. Keep practicing!

You may want to discuss their reports with the children first, then request that they not open them before they reach home. This will prevent discussions and comparisons along the way and might lessen the insensitive competitiveness that arises among children. The feeling of failure that can develop as the children interpret such comments as *Not as good as . . .* , *Having trouble with . . .* , *Not doing well enough to . . .* , or *Isn't able to . . .* will be eliminated. Even that much will be a step forward in changing the focus of school marks from passing and failing to learning. Report cards should be looked forward to, not feared.

If for some reason you have to send home a standard report card, send it along with a written report. In fact you may find the number/grade report easier to fill out when you have the children's work and your anecdotal records to refer to. You may also find that you're focusing more on long-term progress. Include a few words to the parents about how to interpret the report and how to discuss it with their children. Emphasize that a school report is a personal communication between the parents, the teacher and the child.

If you aren't satisfied with the report cards you're being asked to use, make your dissatisfaction and concerns known. Ask *why* they're being used. Ask your administrator or supervisor of curriculum to try to do something about the situation. Be prepared to explain why you feel such reports aren't satisfactory, and if possible, to offer an alternative. Suggest that a committee of teachers be formed to look into the problem and offer solutions. You may not be able to bring changes about immediately, but if you're willing to explain your concerns, you'll be making a positive step towards improvement.

Alternatives

The very best way to give parents an understanding of how their children are developing is a parent-teacher conference. No report card can replace the sharing of information that takes place as teacher and parents meet face-to-face: the chance to ask questions and receive immediate answers, the opportunity to look at a child's work while discussing it. Some teachers have extended the once or twice a year scheduled conference to an open invitation to parents to drop in whenever they want to discuss a question or concern. Some set up monthly mini-conferences for parents of particular children.

Teacher/parent dialogue journals can provide another opportunity to communicate about the children's literacy development. They encourage parents to relay any literacy observations they make at home, to pose questions or make comments about their children's work, and to share anecdotes they feel we will enjoy or find useful to our understanding of the children. We've found that the time we spend writing to parents is time well spent. Together we learn a good deal about their children over the year, and our ongoing dialogue is an important factor in the process. Not all parents feel comfortable with journals, but those who do, acknowledge their effectiveness.

We also try to maintain a dialogue with the parents who choose not to write: through special invitations to come in and discuss specific matters, through brief chats as they pick up or deliver their children (or a forgotten lunch), and through phone calls whenever there's something that warrants immediate contact — perhaps some news we want to share about their children's progress, or simply a question about how things have been going since our last conference.

This doesn't require a lot of time. Sure it takes more time than merely filling in the blanks on a report card and meeting with parents twice a year on the scheduled parents' night. But it's not an unbearable burden. The benefits are well worth it. From the parents we get a much clearer understanding of the children, the environment they live in, and the kind of support they receive at home. And in return we provide the parents with a progressive picture of their children's development, as well as an insight into our classroom program and how they can support it in their homes.

By building such a relationship we solve many of the problems that poor communication can lead to before they have a chance to develop. Continuous reporting over time is far more manageable and sensible than trying to sum up months of development on a single page, or even worse, with a set of letter abbreviations.

Afterword: evaluation and curriculum planning

While discussing evaluation, we would be remiss if we didn't consider how our ideas about evaluation techniques and tools have influenced our role as teachers.

Our decision to become observers and recorders of information has given us a new freedom and responsibility. Our collected information allows us to develop curriculum for the class as a whole as well as for individual children. We see the need for specific types of interaction or intervention, both for individuals and for groups of children. We recognize the necessity of planning specific demonstrations or conferences to focus on a particular strategy or process — although sometimes we decide not to do anything at the moment but watch for further developments. We are able to determine areas of high interest or expertise to encourage and develop. Because we're making observations continuously, we can capitalize immediately on the children's curiosity about a certain topic. We can make invitations and suggestions — possible activities, books to read, people to talk to — at a time when they are most beneficial and apt to be acted upon. The effect of our files and logs is evident in the way we plan for both short-term and long-term growth.

What we learn through our observations gives us insight into the needs of our children, leading us to reflect on the effectiveness of our classroom procedures and program. We begin to question why things we expect to happen aren't happening, or why we see things we don't expect to see. How our reflections may lead to classroom change we can't say. But we know it's impossible to evaluate children's progress by focusing on the children only. We also have to consider the effectiveness of our role in the children's learning, and how we can best promote its development. And in doing so, we sometimes find it necessary to rethink our curriculum planning.

Ultimately, the responsibility for evaluation and for classroom curriculum lies with classroom teachers. We have the power to develop curriculum and make daily decisions which affect the children within our classes, based on our evaluation of the development of our children's literacy skills and the progress the children make on a daily, weekly, monthly basis. We — you! — are the only ones who can make detailed observations that demonstrate growth over time. Only you can recommend the intervention procedures appropriate for a particular child. You may need to call on help, since no teacher knows all there is to know about literacy learning, but ultimately it falls to you to make the best decision possible given the data you've faithfully recorded. Evaluation and curriculum planning don't belong in anyone else's hands. They rightfully belong in yours.

Bibliography

Books and articles

Baskwill, Jane and Paulette Whitman. *Whole Language Sourcebook*. Toronto: Scholastic-TAB Publications Ltd., 1986.

Butler, Andrea and Jan Turnbill. *Towards a Reading and Writing Classroom*. Auckland: Primary English Teachers Association, 1984.

Calkins, Lucy McCormick. *The Art of Teaching Writing*. Portsmouth: Heinemann Educational Books, 1986.

Canfield, Jack and Harold C. Wells. *100 ways to enhance self-concept in the classroom*. New Jersey: Prentice-Hall Inc, 1976.

Clay, Marie. *SAND, a Diagnostic Survey: Concepts about Print Test*. Auckland: Heinemann Educational Books, 1982.

Cochrane, Cochrane, Scalena and Buchanan. *Reading, Writing and Caring*. Winnipeg: Whole Language Consultants Ltd., 1984. (Available in the United States through Richard Owen Inc.)

Goodman, Yetta and Carolyn Burke. *Reading Miscue Inventory Manual: Procedures for Diagnosis and Evaluation*. New York: Macmillan Publishing Co., 1972.

Graves, Donald. *Writing: Teachers and Children at Work*. Portsmouth: Heinemann Educational Books, 1983.

Holdaway, Don. *Independence in Reading: A Handbook on Individualized Procedures*. Sydney: Ashton Scholastic Pty Ltd., 1980.

Jaggar, Angela and Trika Smith-Burke, eds. *Observing the Language Learner*. Urbana, Ill: International Reading Association and National Council of Teachers of English, 1985.

Rowe, Gaelena and Bill Lomas. *A Writing Curriculum Process and Conference*. New York: Oxford University Press, 1985.

Van Manen, Max. *The Tone of Teaching*. Toronto: Scholastic-TAB Publications Ltd, 1986. (Available in the United States through Heinemann Educational Books.)

Journals and newsletters

Highway One, published by the Canadian Council of Teachers of English (CCTE).

"Impressions," a bulletin from Holt Rinehart and Winston.

Language Arts, published by the National Council of Teachers of English (NCTE).

The Reading Teacher, published by the International Reading Association (IRA).

"Whole Language," a newsletter from Scholastic.

Other newsletters are put out by professional associations such as local IRA councils, teacher networks such as TAWL, and the Center for Establishing Dialogue in Teaching and Learning (Box 25170, Tempe, Arizona, 85282).

Titles in the New Directions series

Each book in the New Directions series deals with a single, practical classroom topic or concern, teaching strategy or approach. Many teachers have recognized the collegial and encouraging tone in them — not surprising, since most of them have been written by practicing teachers. Indeed, if you have an idea for a New Directions title of your own, we encourage you to contact the Publishing Division, Scholastic Canada.

Existing titles include:

In Canada, order from: Scholastic-TAB Publications Ltd.,
123 Newkirk Road, Richmond Hill, ON L4C 3G5

In the United States, order from: Scholastic Inc., Box 7502,
Jefferson City, MO 65102